The Everlasting Arms

An Introduction to Best Bereavement and Funeral Practice

David Schofield

THE EVERLASTING ARMS
An Introduction to Best Bereavement and Funeral Practice

Copyright © 2012 David Schofield
Original edition published in English under the title THE EVERLASTING ARMS by Kevin Mayhew Ltd, Buxhall, England.
This edition copyright © Fortress Press 2019

All rights reserved. Except for brief quotations in critical articles or reviews, no part of this book may be reproduced in any manner without prior written permission from the publisher. Email copyright@augsburgfortress.org or write to Permissions, Fortress Press, PO Box 1209, Minneapolis, MN 55440-1209.

Scripture quotations are taken from the HOLY BIBLE, NEW INTERNATIONAL VERSION. Copyright © 1973, 1978, 1984 by International Bible Society. Used by permission of Hodder & Stoughton, a member of the Hodder Headline Group. All rights reserved. "NIV" is a trademark of International Bible Society. UK trademark number 1448790.

Scripture quotations are also taken from The New Revised Standard Version of the Bible, copyright © 1989 by The Division of Christian Education of the National Council of Churches in the USA. Used by permission. All rights reserved.

Cover image: Photo by Henrik Donnestad on unsplash
Cover design: Joe Reinke

Print ISBN: 978-1-5064-5963-9

Dedicated to the many bereaved families to whom I've had the privilege of ministering

Contents

About the Author	6
Introduction	7
1. Attachment and Loss	11
2. The Minister's Point of View	15
3. The Funeral and the Post-Funeral Visit	21
4. Funeral Emotions	27
5. Different Bereavement Situations	35
6. Infant and Childhood Bereavement	41
7. Today's Funeral	45
8. Today's Response	51
Postscript	57
Afterword	60
Further Reading	61
Words of Comfort and Hope: An Anthology of Verse for the Bereaved	63
Options for Pre-Planning a Funeral	73

About the Author

David Schofield is a retired Anglican priest who served all his thirty-two years of ministry in the Diocese of Lincoln. He now lives with his wife of forty-five years, Christine, in the High Peak area of Derbyshire.

David's first book, *Troubled Water*, is his account of how he dealt with his cancer. David was diagnosed in June 2008 with myeloma and since then has sought to try and make sense of his illness and bring something positive from it.

Introduction

The eternal God is your refuge, and underneath are the everlasting arms.
Deuteronomy 33:27 (NIV)

It was Sunday lunchtime and the phone rang. The funeral director informed me that an elderly parishioner had died and that the widow would like a service in church on Wednesday morning. I was a young curate with two full weeks' experience behind me and the vicar was on vacation. My only experience of funerals was as an observer at a service taken by the vicar the week before. What was I to do?

With virtually no real training in the conduct of funerals and even less in grief counseling, there was only one thing that I could do – *panic!* No. Like most inexperienced clergy faced with this situation and with no help at hand, I set off to visit the widow, relying entirely on common sense and praying for a great deal of help from the Almighty.

Happily, the visit and the funeral both went off without a hitch, but I'm convinced that I received much more help from that widow than ever she did from me. I owe her a great deal.

After many hundreds of similar occasions, I now feel able to offer some help to those (both newly-ordained clergy and lay people) who find themselves involved in arranging and/or taking funerals.

For over thirty years I have, like my fellow clergy, been heavily involved in taking funeral services and all the concomitant work. I have always found this to be deeply satisfying and from it I have developed an interest in grief and bereavement. For some years I acted as support coordinator for a Cruse Bereavement counseling group. Extensive reading over the years has given me some insight into this fascinating subject.

Over those thirty years of my ministry I have

had conversations with funeral directors from the diocese of Lincoln in which I served and these, together with my own experiences, reading, and shared experiences from other clergy, caused me to consider some of the modern trends in funeral practice.

But first, a word of warning: no amount of what my grandfather called "book learning" can ever be a substitute for experience. Reading this will not necessarily make you an expert grief counselor or funeral officiant, but it will, I hope, help you to avoid some of the pitfalls. It may also help to enable you to offer constructive counsel to those to whom you are called to minister.

My aim in this book is to offer some advice to those who are called upon to officiate at funerals and to offer some insight to those interested in bereavement care. The book also considers some of the modern trends attached to grieving, especially where these involve people on the fringe of the Church and those with little or no Christian affiliation. Many of such people will have their own implicit spirituality, what one might, without any pejorative connotation, term "folk religion." It is not my intention to provide answers to all the questions raised, but rather to leave some questions open for discussion as to how we, the Church, might incorporate these practices and bring some distinctly Christian spirituality to these "fringe funerals."

First I shall look briefly at what bereavement means, then discuss ways in which those who officiate might proceed. Further chapters look at the feelings of the officiant and how the funeral can be an aid to the grieving process. They discuss some of the particularities of various bereavement situations including infant and childhood bereavement, multiple deaths, and community grief. Finally, I shall seek to highlight the implicit religion contained in some modern funeral practices and grieving processes and look at the Church's response to implicit religion in funerals and ask how we might introduce the Christian message within this context.

INTRODUCTION

I write from the perspective of the Anglican Church, and in discussing funeral services specific reference will be made to the forms of service authorized by the Church of England. Readers from other denominations will, I trust, be able to relate points made there to aspects of their own authorized services. In the main I have used the general term "(funeral) minister" for those conducting funeral services or caring pastorally for the bereaved, and have indicated when this is a lay person.

One

Attachment and Loss

Throughout our lives we are all faced with what we might term "loss situations," when someone or something to which we have become attached is, in one way or another, taken from us. Such losses include a wide variety of situations, such as: the death of a pet; the temporary loss of a keepsake; a child starting school for the first time, or going off to college, or leaving home; losing a job; divorce; moving; or even the loss of one's youth.

These situations may seem trivial to the outsider, but to those immediately involved, they are real loss situations and as such involve a form of grief and require a degree of mourning and adjustment. We need to express these feelings of sadness and loss and this is the perfectly natural process that we call grief. Whatever the loss situation, it is important to acknowledge that a change has taken place. Something once cherished has been lost and there is sadness at its passing.

It is helpful to draw a subtle difference between grief and mourning. For the purposes of clarity I would describe grief as "that personal feeling of loss that comes when we are deprived of something we value: a sense of emptiness and intense sadness." Mourning, on the other hand, I would describe as "the way we deal with that grief." This is the outward and social aspect that we bring to bear on our grief in order to make it slightly more bearable.

We can see, then, that attachment and loss are but two sides of the same coin. Love and grief go hand in hand. I suggest that we only grieve for the loss of what is valued. Others may see that "value" as insignificant but it is not so to the person concerned. Just as the degree of value and attachment differs, so does the sense of loss.

In a way, grief is the price we pay for loving. One of the many platitudes that is often directed at people who are grieving is that "time is a great healer." However well meaning this may be, it doesn't really bring much comfort. Time indeed *is* a great healer, but it doesn't erase the scars of bereavement. At the time of bereavement, the future can be a very distant place and any thought of "feeling better" may seem impossible. Even years afterward, the still-painful memories can remain.

It is important to realize that the grief of a bereaved partner (and I use this term to denote wife, husband, or partner – whether recognized by a civil ceremony or not) is just as real as the grief experienced by, say, a grandchild on the death of a grandparent. Only the intensity is different. It is also important to realize that the lack of any outward sign of grief does not necessarily mean that there is a lack of attachment. Neither does the lack of attachment mean that there will be little sense of loss or grief on the death of another.

> William and Mary gave the impression of having a rather less than ideal relationship. Each would constantly complain of the other's lack of consideration. They appeared to be in conflict at every point. Many among their friends and family thought that when Mary died, William would not be too upset by his loss. The reverse was in fact the case: he had lost his partner of over sixty years and his grief was commensurate with so many years of married life. Within a matter of months, William, too, had died.

One of the first things we have to realize is that everyone grieves in their own way – there is no set model for grief. We cannot and must not say that at any given time all bereaved people will be at a particular stage of mourning. Each individual forms their own pattern of grief and displays it, or withholds it, in their own way. One person can present a very stoical face to the world in the presence of their grief, while another will openly display tears and other such outward signs of grief. The behavior of the bereaved can depend on their temperament, the degree of attachment to the deceased, and also on the age of the deceased. At the death of an older person who has lived a long and good life, there is often a sense of fulfillment while for someone who dies young, or as a child, there is the grieving for the life that has never been lived.

Not everyone is able to "put on a brave face" and some prefer to remain at home in the safety of familiar surroundings where they can express their grief alone. Others try stoically to carry on in as near a normal way as possible. Both of these attitudes are right, as there is no right or wrong way of grieving or mourning. It can be a little counterproductive to talk in terms of "stages" of grief, as each person has to grieve in their own unique way. I prefer to think in terms of "aspects" of grief. A primary care physician; or, doctor; or, physician friend once described it this way: "Grief is not so much a die-cast model car, which is shaped to a preordained design but more of one built to one's own specification out of building bricks, picking and choosing the various aspects that best suit our own situation and temperament."

It is not unusual for some people to demonstrate a variety of emotions all at the same time. There are some people who appear to follow the classic traits of numbness, anxiety, guilt, anger, and sadness, while others do not. Some people may experience a very real sense of the presence of the deceased and such hallucinations can be very comforting. At other times or to other people these could cause distress. It should be remembered that none of these experiences should be regarded as "wrong," but rather as an individual expression of grief. There are many books available on varying grief patterns.

Two

The Minister's Point of View

Much has been written, by a variety of authors, about the psychology of grief and there are deep theological implications when we begin to think and talk about *life after death* or *eternal life*, or any other term we may choose to describe what happens after death. I do not intend here to delve too deeply into these particular areas but I would recommend funeral ministers taking time to read some of the excellent work that is available on these aspects.

In my experience, the majority of bereaved families that we meet, are not necessarily *church-going* Christian families. One of the things that we have to consider is the application of our own theology. An important watchword is *Beware of jargon!* For example, to talk with the bereaved in terms that would satisfy a theologian, may only serve to confuse and bewilder those who have little or no Christian background. We need, therefore, to be aware of our own priorities, deciding for ourselves what we envisage our task to be in these loss situations. Our task is to minister to the bereaved in a way that is both meaningful and acceptable to them while at the same time not compromising our own faith. The example of Jesus on the road to Emmaus (Luke 24:13-32) serves to remind us that Jesus met people where they were on their journey and traveled with them. So we, too, should be prepared to meet the bereaved wherever they might be on their journey of faith and life, and travel some of that journey with them.

Just as there is no set pattern to grief, so there is no set pattern for ministering to the bereaved. Each bereaved person has a unique relationship with the deceased and each one has their own interpretation of what is involved, spiritually, with death. It is to this unique understanding that we are called to minister. This can, at first, appear to be a rather daunting task.

To help this I shall follow through the various stages of preparing for and arranging a funeral, as they occur in a bereavement situation. But first, a word of warning: in no way can these thoughts be taken as a set model for all events. The stages through which our task moves can roughly be categorized as: *request for a service and the initial visit*, which I shall talk about in this chapter, and *the funeral and the post-funeral visit*, which will be in the following one.

Request for a service

Obviously, this varies from parish to parish and from funeral director to funeral director. Usually the initial contact comes through the funeral director, although for members of our congregation this might come direct from the family. In many cases the funeral director arranges the time and date with the family and then confirms this with the minister. Some of the more enlightened funeral directors will check the availability of the minister and the church before committing to a date and time but, sadly, this is often not the case.

The funeral director can be a valuable source of information about the deceased person and their family and we would do well to cultivate good relations with our local funeral director. It is always worthwhile gleaning as much background information as possible before making the initial contact with the family. If we can build up a mental picture of the deceased and their relationship with the bereaved, then we will be better able to come close to the family in their bereavement.

Details available from the funeral director might include: full names; date, place, and time of death; cause of death; marital status, family details; occupation; and any involvement the deceased may have had in the local community. We shall also have details of what type of service is required: church service with cremation or burial, or some other combination; whether hymns have already been chosen; and any other initial decisions made by the family.

Some clergy and lay ministers feel that it is not the funeral director's task to elicit details of the service, but they are very experienced professionals and are usually very capable and sympathetic to the idiosyncrasies of the local funeral ministers.

Armed with this valuable background information, we are ready to make the initial visit.

The initial visit

There are no "ground rules" for funeral visits, but there are some points that are worth noting.

1. Be identifiable. An increasing number of clergy feel that it is not always necessary in general ministry to wear the "collar," but in situations like this it is always a good idea to wear a clerical collar. This makes us immediately identifiable for what and who we are. For the lay funeral minister, some form of identification is essential, especially in this present age with so many bogus officials trying to dupe the unwary. Having some form of immediate identification can also offer to the bereaved family a point of reference, indicating authority and security at a very bewildering time. We need to remember that to many non-church people, the vicar or lay funeral minister is an unknown quantity – a strange creature – outside their usual circle of acquaintances.

2. Don't wait too long. The initial visit cannot be made too close to the time of death. It is often thought that families need time to come to terms with their loss before we appear on their doorstep and that too soon a visit could seem cold and heartless. This is often the thinking of a fearful visitor. We may be projecting our apprehension onto the bereaved family. Our task is to minister to the bereaved and it is essential to make an early identification with their grief. We need to remember that our prime objective is *not* just arranging the funeral – it is ministering to the bereaved! It is possible that during the initial visit, no mention of the service is made. If that is where the family are then that is the right thing to do. A

second visit is often necessary to discuss details of the service. The family often want an opportunity to talk about the deceased, sometimes amid tears. Allow them that opportunity and allow them to cry. While tears may be embarrassing to us, they can be very cathartic. If appropriate offer a hand to hold or a shoulder to cry on. But in this increasingly politically correct world we need to be very careful about physical contact. Also allow for times of silence. Don't try to fill up every space in the conversation with words. Sometimes the silence is a time of recollection and remembering.

3. Be sensitive. So often the cold, bald statement on the doorstep: *I'm Joe Bloggs, I understand that your husband/wife has just died* will be too stark and might only serve to upset or even antagonize, and be seen as insensitive. Sad to say, there are still many who adopt the "business-like" approach to funeral visiting, complete with a checklist of what information is required. Usually, seeing the vicar on the doorstep is enough to indicate the purpose of the visit. For the lay funeral minister, simply saying that you are from the (local) church and have come to offer the Church's condolences will be enough to gain admission. Don't be too eager to steer the conversation around to the details of the funeral, allow the family to set its own agenda and timescale on this. General conversation and the retelling of the story of the bereavement often reveal quite a lot about the deceased and their relationships. Hints picked up in this way can then be fed back into the conversation and be a help in correcting the mental picture that we had previously formed. It is, of course, necessary to check details and make definite arrangements, but these can be done sensitively and without running through a checklist. We would do well to cultivate a memory that holds on to essential details in order to record them later, maybe even in the car outside immediately after the visit. Avoid referring to the deceased as "your *late* wife/husband" because, to the bereaved, that relationship to the deceased still exists and to keep their name in the present tense can have

the added effect of softening the starkness of the bereavement situation.

4. Be prepared for questions. The bereaved often have a number of questions they wish to ask and they may not all be directly related to our sphere of work. We need to be honest enough to admit that we don't always have the answers. Questions such as: "Why did he have to die?" or "Why her and not me?" or "Why did God take him?" have no ready answer and this is not the appropriate time to indulge in deep theological debate. Admit that we don't know and that we, like them, are perplexed by the question.

Other questions, which we do feel able to deal with, might concern tradition, or practice, or practicalities: should black clothes be worn; should children be allowed to attend the funeral; do I have to see them in the coffin; and other such practical questions. Again, to these questions there are no set answers. Everything depends on the individual bereaved person and strict adherence to local or family traditions is not always helpful; indeed they can be distressing.

On two specific questions I offer the following considerations:

Do I have to see them in the coffin?

Having been able to view the body can be a great comfort to the bereaved in the later stages of grief. This is especially true where the death occurred away from home with no family member present (for example, in the emergency room after an accident or sudden death). Although the visit to the Chapel of Rest may be initially distressing, it can enable the bereaved to accept the fact of death and can help to avoid that sense of "it didn't really happen."

However, the viewing of the body can have the converse effect. For some people, seeing a loved one lying in their coffin may be very distressing for a variety of reasons. Sometimes the reason is fear, both real and imaginary and we must be guided by the wishes of the bereaved. If necessary, be prepared to accompany them to view the body.

Should children be allowed to attend the funeral?
I believe that this depends on their age and whether they wish to attend. No pressure should be brought to bear on them either to go or stay away. They, too, have their grief, which they may or may not know how to deal with. We must remember not to ignore the children. They can feel very much alone when all the attention is centered on the parent(s), especially in the instance of the death of a sibling. Parents are often too distressed themselves to be able to offer support to their children at a time when it is very much needed.

5. It may well be necessary for us to spread these tasks over two or more visits; only the experience of the moment can decide. We have to remember that we are dealing with adults, but ones who, for one reason or another, need to be approached as if they were in a child-like situation, if we are to help them through a potentially stressful and intensely emotional period. Above all, be guided by the situation, as no two people deal with grief and bereavement in the same way.

6. Please be aware that caring for the bereaved can be mentally straining and stressful to those who minister to them. It can be helpful to talk of these stresses and strains to one's partner or to a fellow minister, allowing always that we maintain the boundaries of confidentiality.

Three

The Funeral and the Post-Funeral Visit

The next and most important event is the funeral itself. This may take a variety of forms: a church service followed by burial or cremation; a service in a cemetery chapel or by the graveside; a service in the crematorium chapel. Our conduct and that of the funeral director, will be of the greatest importance to the bereaved family and, indeed, to the other mourners present. The choice of time, date, and venue will have already been decided, but the choice of service, with exception of hymns, is often left entirely to the minister, although an increasing number of families do have some input to make. We need to be open to the wishes of the bereaved and try to help them devise a service whose content is both liturgically sound and pastorally sensitive. There may well be a wish to include live or recorded music that has a special significance to the bereaved or the deceased and we do need to be sensitive and nonjudgmental in our approach to this area.

The form of service used is often left to the minister and there are strong arguments in the Anglican tradition, for both the Book of Common Prayer (BCP) and Common Worship (CW). The BCP has the benefit of well-loved and remembered words and phrases, while CW has a more modern language, which can be most sensitive and helpful. Never be afraid of adapting either, or both, to suit the occasion. Only beware of having minds closed to the advantages of either service.

CW provides for the use of the deceased's name in the prayers, which can have the effect of making the service even more personal. It is important, therefore, that we use the correct name. This might sound obvious, but not everyone uses his or her given name. We need to ascertain from the family which name the deceased used. This may be a diminutive or nickname and should only be used with the family's permission, as it could well be too intimate for general usage. It seems important to me that we use the deceased's full name at the beginning of the service in order to put the whole service into context.

In general practice, an address is often included in the funeral service and we would do well to follow the advice given by the Liturgical Committee in the commentary on the Alternative Service Book (ASB), which suggests that the sermon "ought in any case to be brief for the sake of the mourners." A brief comment on the Christian teaching about death and resurrection can be helpful, but lengthy eulogies by the minister should be avoided. Any "life history" should be brief and, ideally, given by a family member or friend. I have found that reading 1 Corinthians chapter 13, and then commenting on the eternal nature of God's love, can be very helpful and comforting to the bereaved. It should always be remembered that it is to the bereaved that we are ministering at this traumatic time.

The BCP directs that the minister shall meet the body "at the entrance to the churchyard." This is a valuable practice as it identifies the minister with both the deceased and the family. Try to maintain this identification by adjusting the pace of the cortege to that of the slowest mourner. Nothing is more unseemly than the minister walking yards ahead of the coffin and mourners. Once inside the church (or crematorium chapel) try to stand in a position where you can see, and be seen by, the chief mourners. A minister hidden behind a pillar, or a rood screen, can have the effect of making them seem detached from the proceedings. As a general rule, I stand on the chancel step at the foot of the coffin for most of the service in church and move to the head of the coffin, facing the altar, for the prayers. The overall watchword should be sensitivity.

Except where the whole service is taken in the crematorium chapel, the committal is separated from the main service. Try to make the committal short but without indecent brevity. I find the blessing of the congregation after the committal marks the closure of the funeral ceremonies. In some cases the family ask to have the committal before the church service and this changes the whole complexion of the service. The church service then is more of a celebration of the life of the deceased; a form of memorial service.

Our task is to conduct the funeral in a dignified and sensitive way, but occasionally outside events intrude on this. In thirty years of ministry, I have experienced irrational behavior by mourners; a grave dug to the wrong size; a mourner collapsing in the churchyard; and an organist having a heart attack at the beginning of the service. Dealing with the irrational behavior of mourners is generally seen as the responsibility of the funeral director. In the case where the grave was dug to the wrong size, I explained to the family that we would go ahead with the committal but with the coffin still at the side of the grave. I would then wait with the body until the grave had been altered and the coffin respectfully interred. This meant that the mourners didn't have to witness the gravedigger trying to dig the grave to the right size.

There is no panacea for dealing with these or any other emergency, only the sensitivity and experience of the minister and funeral director working together.

Leave-taking at the end of a service can sometimes be difficult and I tend to adopt the following criteria: after interment in the cemetery or churchyard, allow mourners time alone by the graveside, waiting by the churchyard gate or by the cars to bid farewell as they leave. After a service or committal at the crematorium, bid farewell at the chapel door and allow the family time alone to view the flowers and talk to family and friends.

Finally, two words of warning: first, don't say that you will stop by and see the family again if you do not intend, or will not have the time to do so. Secondly, when, or if, you are thanked for your services, try to avoid the rather unfortunate "it was a pleasure." A simple "thank you" is sufficient.

I realize some of these points seem obvious but I feel they are worth reminding ourselves of them.

The post-funeral visit

This is one area where the clergy often have difficulty. The demands made upon our time often make a post-funeral visit an added chore, which tends to be put off or forgotten. If we are to minister fully to the bereaved, it is an essential part of our work. The timing of this visit needs to be considered separately for each family. It may be right to visit the following day and in some cases every few days for a while. Sometimes the following week is early enough, or even after some longer time. If the widowed person has had family or friends staying, there will be a strong framework of support and it could be more helpful to leave the post-funeral visit until they have left. Immediately following a death there is quite often that strong framework of support from family, friends, and neighbors. After a while this begins to diminish and if we are aware of this, then as the framework is being withdrawn it might be a suitable time for the visit.

If the parish has a network of parish visitors, this is one area in which they might well be engaged. If no such network exists, it is worth considering setting one up. As the purpose of this visit is to offer help to the bereaved in working out their grief feelings, it would be helpful if the visitors were given some basic training in bereavement work. The feelings of the bereaved can take many forms: shock, numbness, anger, guilt, or anxiety. A useful book on this subject is *Through Grief*, by Elizabeth Collick *(Darton, Longman & Todd, 1986)*.

As clergy, we do not always feel equipped to deal with any positive bereavement counseling and it is important to recognize this. Acknowledging our own inability is *not* failure but an honest admission of our limitations. We should never be afraid to be "stretcher-bearers"; that is, to recognize a situation that needs professional help and to steer the bereaved in the direction of qualified help. CRUSE, the organization for the care of the bereaved, is well equipped in this field of grief counseling, as is the Society of Compassionate Friends and other such organizations. These organizations are usually willing to share their expertise and help with training parish visitors.

Four
Funeral Emotions

The funeral as an aid to grieving

We all need to mark significant events in life with some kind of rite or ceremony. In all religions, even among the most primitive peoples, there are rites and ceremonies attendant upon birth, puberty, marriage, and death: rites of welcome, of celebration, of union, and of farewell. At its most basic level, a funeral is a form of ritual farewell, marking the end of a stage in life for both the bereaved and the deceased. Putting aside any specific Christian content, the funeral makes a public statement that the life of the deceased is over, and making such a statement can help the bereaved toward admitting the fact of death and their own changed status. This can be a significant step on the path toward acceptance and closure.

For many people the arranging of a funeral can be a very painful and traumatic exercise at an emotionally difficult time: a time when they don't really feel like making any decisions at all. There is, however, within that pain, a sense of catharsis, which can aid the grieving process. The arrangement of some form of funeral service, be it in church or in a cemetery or crematorium chapel, can fulfill the need for positive action. Not everyone is psychologically ready to undertake detailed arrangements and this is an area in which the experience of a funeral director is most helpful. But often there is the feeling of a need to "do something"; and the making of the necessary funeral arrangements can provide an outlet for this need. The bereaved can, in this way, feel that they are "doing something" for the deceased.

The actual details of the funeral are very often decided on by following the wishes of the deceased and by tradition and/or local custom. It is much more difficult for families to make funeral arrangements when the subject has never been talked about. I have always encouraged people to make some decisions, however tentative, while still in good health. In some parishes, clergy have devised a simple form for parishioners to outline details of what they would like for their funerals. These, where used, have been very helpful to the families when death finally happens. I have provided an example of one such form at the end of the book (see pages 73-76).

Having this kind of skeletal framework in which to make the arrangements can help to give a sense of security or rightness to the occasion. In making the arrangements and in the funeral itself, there can be a certain palliative quality, which can be an aid to the grieving process.

As well as being a form of ritual farewell for the next of kin and close family, the funeral can give an opportunity for friends, neigbors, fellow workers, and acquaintances to say farewell and to express their own grief. It can also be helpful to the bereaved to know just how much the deceased was loved and valued within the community. This expression of love, respect, and worth is, to some extent, also directed toward the bereaved. Some of the mourners at the funeral may well be present in order to express their love of and respect for the bereaved. To know and feel this community support can be of great value and help at a very difficult time.

Just as the funeral makes a public statement about the fact of death, so also it gives, in some sense, permission for the bereaved to display their grief. It is not considered improper, or wrong, or selfish to display their sense of loss on the occasion of the funeral. There are some mourners, however, who feel that they have to maintain the "stiff upper lip" tradition and feel unable to "let go" and express some of their grief. Yet within this "safe" environment it can be another valuable aid to the grieving process. This public statement about their loss and grief can have a cathartic and healing quality.

Within the context of a Christian funeral (as with other religions) there is also an expression of hope: the hope and belief that death is but the gateway to eternal life – another plane of being – however we interpret it. With a few exceptions, most people have some concept of "life after death," however basic this might be. This continuance of life after death is part of the traditional Christian concept, and there are numerous interpretations of this within the various Christian traditions. For some it might just be something as vague as the one who has died being "with God," or that they live on in their offspring. However life after death is perceived, to have the reassurance of such continuance can have a palliative effect. The pain of the final permanence of death, on a purely physical level, is eased by this hope and expectation of a spiritual continuance.

Within this context of hope, remembrance can play an important part. For some it will be a bittersweet experience, reminding them of their loss and, at the same time, assuring them of the concept of continuance. This is often expressed by the bereaved in visiting the grave, taking flowers to the crematorium, or laying flowers by the roadside or place of death on anniversaries or birthdays. (See Chapter 7 on "Today's funeral.")

The Church can have a valuable role in this area of remembrance; a role which can also be both an opportunity for teaching the Christian belief in resurrection and for offering comfort to the bereaved.

A simple annual memorial service, held at All Souls' or All Saints' tide, to which those who have been bereaved in the past year can be invited, can be an aid to remembering and to mutual sharing of grief. In some churches contributions, in a loved one's name, toward the cost of the Easter flowers or candles at Christmas, are invited and a list of names is displayed or read out at the appropriate services. In traditions where prayers for the departed are not usual, the imaginative use of thanksgiving and prayers for the bereaved can be helpful within a context similar to the memorial service, offering thanks for the lives lived and the loves shared, and praying for God's help and comfort for the bereaved. Letting the bereaved family know that the local church will be praying for them and remembering their loved one on the Sunday before and/or following the funeral can also be very comforting. A simple card bearing this information and the time and date of the service, given to the family at the initial visit, can be helpful. (See the sample funeral visit card on page 76.)

The funeral and any consequent act of remembrance on the part of the Church, can be an opportunity to offer comfort and support to the bereaved and, if these services are used in a sensitive and imaginative way, can be an important aid in the grieving process.

The helpers and their feelings

It is not just the bereaved who can find funerals emotional and challenging; the officiating minister also has to deal with his or her own emotions. We may have known the deceased and as such we have our own grief to consider as well as that of the family. There is a need to balance this with our ability to minister to them.

The subtle balance of detachment, sympathy, empathy, and compassion which is needed in ministering to the bereaved, really only comes by experience and cannot be taught or learned. Sympathy and compassion are much alike: the wish to ease the pain and to help and support, coupled with a feeling of understanding the other's pain. This desire to comfort and help comes easily to most people and is often the beginning of the "helping" situation. Very often the motivation to be involved in caregiving work stems from a sense of compassion and sympathy with those who suffer.

Empathy, however, is a more demanding emotion and only comes through mental effort and experience. It is the taking upon oneself the feelings of the bereaved; an attempt to put oneself in their position and so trying to feel what they might be feeling. The difference between sympathy and empathy has been described thus: sympathy is seeing a person who has fallen down a hole and feeling sorry for them, while empathy is getting into the hole with them to help them. This is never an easy task and can be mentally very demanding.

The sense of failure to cure and inadequacy to avert death is especially predominant with healthcare workers. They are often expected by society to be the ones who are able to avoid the death of their patients by use of their medico-surgical expertise. When a death does occur, there is a tendency to feel that they have failed to fulfill their task.

A sense of having failed is, of course, natural and acceptable, but to emphasize this into a sense of failure – complete failure – is both unwise and counterproductive. Taken to the extreme this could lead to an inability or unwillingness to continue in the caregiving profession and has occasionally resulted in the loss of a good and dedicated healthcare worker. This being said, a sense of inadequacy can be a positive attribute as it is important to realize our own limitations.

Clergy too can sometimes have this sense of having failed, especially if they have been praying for an individual's healing and that person then dies. I would suggest that death is not seen as failure but rather as the ultimate healing. The verb "to heal" has its roots in the Old English word meaning to be whole. Wholeness, understood as being at one with God, is therefore the epitome of healing.

The effect of involvement in the events surrounding a death can have a draining effect on us and leave us feeling mentally exhausted. There is a need to unwind after such involvement, especially if further caregiving work is to be done for someone else immediately afterward. This is particularly true for the medical profession and for clergy. A helper who is as distraught as the bereaved is of very little help. Maintaining a degree of professional detachment is important yet we must beware of such detachment turning into, or being perceived as, callousness. While a degree of detachment is essential if we are to be of any real help to the bereaved, this must always be tempered with compassion. Sometimes detachment is used to mask our sense of inadequacy; we think (and sometimes actually say) "It's not my problem," or "It has nothing to do with me," or "I'm only here to conduct the funeral." Obviously this kind of detachment is to be deplored in those in the caregiving professions.

We are regularly placed in positions where we have to minister to the bereaved and, almost immediately afterward, face a completely different pastoral situation. It is not helpful to either party to take the pain of bereavement into other pastoral situations. We need, therefore, to cultivate the ability to remain detached while, at the same time, being fully sympathetic and compassionate.

Not everyone has an inborn, natural ability to deal with bereavement situations and there is no disgrace in accepting one's inability to cope with these. When this is the case, our task is that of "stretcher-bearer." That is to say we need to pass on the bereaved person to someone who is more able to help. A basic training in bereavement care can enable those who feel uncertain, to fulfill their "stretcher-bearing" role more effectively.

For many people, being present at a death is not something with which they are familiar and, as such, they are rather nervous about the whole death experience. In my own ministry I have been with people only moments before their death and with families immediately after a death, but it wasn't until three years before retirement that I was actually present at the moment of death. All my past experience of bereavement care seemed to be validated by this one event. This was the death of my own mother and, as such, it was a privilege to experience it.

Only when we have come to terms with our own feelings, can we begin to fulfill a useful ministry to the bereaved. We do not have to have experienced death personally in order to understand our own feelings but we do need to have addressed those feelings. We advise the bereaved to discuss their feelings of loss, openly, with family and friends and, similarly, it is very helpful for us to discuss our personal feelings with others in the same, or a similar, profession. It may even be that on occasion we do not really appreciate what our feelings are until we vocalize them in the presence of a sympathetic listener. Putting our thoughts and feelings into words, spoken or written, can be very cathartic.

Five

Different Bereavement Situations

No two bereavement situations are the same; they are as different as are the people involved in them. But it may be helpful to look briefly at some of the bereavements that I have encountered in my ministry. These are not offered as definitive answers on how to deal with the situations, but rather they are offered to share with the reader how I have approached them. The death of someone is always traumatic and painful, even after an illness or after a reasonably long life when death might be expected, but some situations require a slightly different approach.

Bereavement as a result of a road accident

I have been involved in a number of funerals of road accident victims and each one is, of course, different. Generally speaking there is a great sense of being robbed, not only of the person who died, but also of the opportunity to prepare for the death and to say farewell. In the many funerals of road accident victims that I have conducted, I have usually, in the prayers, asked for a time of silence in which the mourners might say to the deceased the things they would have liked to have said to them, had they had the opportunity before their death. This has no theological basis, but does give considerable psychological help and comfort to the bereaved. I have also, on occasion, stood with the family at the site of the road accident and said a prayer. This too has given comfort to those who were present.

Bereavement as a result of suicide

This is a particularly difficult situation and often throws up some very strong feelings in the bereaved. As well as all the usual feelings of grief, there is often anger directed at the deceased for the action they have taken and the resulting effect on the family. There is then a feeling of guilt for feeling that anger. The bereaved need to be allowed to express these feelings without any comment from the one ministering to them. Again, like those who mourn after a road accident, we can allow a time of quiet in the funeral service in which to express silently any feelings that still linger.

Bereavement as a result of murder

Murder, like suicide, is a very emotive subject and, fortunately for me, I have very little firsthand knowledge of its victims. There is the obvious anger against the (known or unknown) perpetrator as well as the added pressure of the intrusion of the news media into the family's private grief. All that has been said about road accidents and suicide applies to these funerals. Depending on how the family feel, there could be an opportunity within the service for some kind of prayer for the perpetrator as well as for the police who may have been instrumental in making the arrest.

Bereavement as a result of service in the armed forces

This bereavement situation is, sadly, becoming more widespread. We do not, as a general rule, have to deal with the repatriation ceremonies of those killed while serving overseas, as this is done by a chaplaincy service. We are, however, called to minister to the families. These funerals involve rather a lot of military ceremony and, usually, the appropriate armed service will either undertake the organizing of them or will help with advice if requested. There is very much a sense of pride as well as grief as families say farewell to someone of whom they are very proud. This too should be acknowledged in both the visiting and in the prayers and address in the service.

Bereavement when mourners are not able to be at the funeral

Sometimes a situation arises where the next of kin is not able to be present at the funeral. One such occurred when the husband died while the wife was seriously ill in the hospital. She was not well enough to leave the hospital for many weeks and it was agreed to go ahead with the funeral which was to be held in a neighboring parish. I arranged with the hospital to be with the widow at the same time that the service was taking place and, together with one of the nurses, we read the funeral service. This was much appreciated by the bereaved family and gave the widow a feeling of being present at the funeral, albeit by proxy.

On another occasion the funeral was to take place in South Africa and many of the family were not able to attend. Again, at the same time as the funeral took place in South Africa, we gathered in the parish church and had a funeral service, albeit without a coffin. Later, some of the deceased's ashes were brought back to the UK and interred in the churchyard.

Bereavement as a result of AIDS

There is still a great deal of fear and misunderstanding about those who suffer from AIDS. I believe that the funeral service should be no different from other funeral services. We need to put aside any preconceived ideas and prejudices we have about the lifestyle of the deceased and remember that to the bereaved family, the deceased was loved for who and what they were. I found it appropriate in one case to use the service to pray for all who suffer from AIDS-related illnesses and for all who minister to them. In another service it would have been inappropriate to do so as the deceased was a prominent local person and their condition wasn't generally known.

Bereavement as a result of a disaster

All bereavement is a disaster to the families concerned, but here I'm thinking about natural or national disasters. Tsunamis, shootings, or fires are examples. As well as the personal grief of the families there is a degree of community or even national grief to consider. In some cases there may have to be a funeral service without a body, as is the case with many tsunami victims. These services need extra thought and the families and funeral minister need to work together to create the service that will truly reflect who and what the deceased was.

Bereavement when there is no family

Only once in my ministry have I been called upon to conduct a funeral service paid for by the local authority where there were no family or friends. It was a sad reflection on the funeral director that the coffin arrived at the cemetery chapel in his van rather than a hearse. He then suggested that as there were no mourners we could just skip the service and proceed to the interment. My personal feeling was that as there was no one to mourn the man's death, then we should do so. The funeral director, the cemetery superintendant, and the grave-digger were the only congregation as we read the burial service and said prayers for the deceased.

Bereavement when the wrong body has been identified

Perhaps one of the more difficult funeral services I have had to conduct was that of a person whose body had been wrongly identified. The deceased had not been seen in the coffin by the family, as they wanted to remember her as she was. It was only when the second family went to see their relative that the mistake was discovered. As we had had one funeral service for the assumed deceased, we had to try to replicate the service for the correct body. There was added distress caused to both families as the second family had to have a funeral service without a body.

Bereavement when the deceased is unloved

It is quite unusual to meet a bereaved family who have so much antipathy toward the deceased that they really do not wish to have a funeral service at all. One such family asked that the body be taken to the crematorium unaccompanied and no service held, as the deceased had been an abusive bully to all of his family. There was a great deal of anger among the bereaved family mixed with a sense of relief that the bully had died. These feelings of anger and relief also had a tinge of guilt. The widow felt torn between wanting to "make sure he's gone" (her words) and not having anything to do with a funeral. We compromised in that we met the coffin at the crematorium and

I simply read the funeral service with no hymns or music and no eulogy or address. Afterward the family expressed their gratitude in that I had encouraged them to make that final gesture of farewell. Overall, it was a very difficult funeral.

Six

Infant and Childhood Bereavement

Infant bereavement (and in this I include miscarriage, stillbirth, termination, and neonatal death) is an area which is often neglected in pastoral work and this is perhaps because of the complex nature of the grief which is involved and a sense of our own inadequacy. It is, for all concerned, a very emotive and traumatic time. Much of what has been said earlier applies equally to infant bereavement.

In the case of miscarriage, stillbirth, or neonatal death, there is a very real need to grieve for the loss of the unborn or newly born child. Happily the attitude of nursing staff and clergy is changing from the "you can always have another baby" to a more sensitive and caring approach. To the parent(s), the dead child was, and is, very much a part of the family. A mother who carries a child in her womb for however long or short a time, has developed some degree of attachment to the child. This child is already part of the family: plans have been made; hopes have been raised; nurseries may have been prepared. Suddenly to find all these preparations to be in vain can cause a great deal of distress to the whole family. It would be insensitive to try to pretend that the baby had never existed. A period of mourning and readjustment is essential

There is quite a lot of ignorance about what is and is not possible with a stillborn baby. Questions are often asked, like: "Can we have a funeral?" or "Does the hospital deal with the burial or cremation of the baby?" The answer is, of course, that the family have the same rights over a stillborn baby as if the child had lived after birth. The parents of a stillborn infant once asked me if they were allowed to attend the funeral of their baby as the hospital was paying for it. This is, sadly, an often-asked question and of course the answer is a definite "yes." There is something very poignant about the funeral of an infant and in seeing that small white coffin as it is lowered into a grave or as the curtains of the crematorium close around it.

I have deliberately included termination of pregnancy (abortion) in this area. There is often a great deal of moral indignation about termination, for whatever reason, and because of this the feelings of the parent(s) are sometimes dismissed. There is a great tendency to place all the responsibility for the termination on the selfishness of the parent(s) without attempting to discover the full facts of the situation, or to understand that there is often another, equally valid, point of view. For many mothers, there is a very real sense of failure after a termination, just as there is after a miscarriage, stillbirth, or neonatal death. Time is needed in which the mother can express and come to terms with her feelings. We need to be able to put aside our prejudices in order to minister fully to the bereaved parents in these situations.

As yet the Church is too divided over the whole subject to be able to offer a form of prayer that would meet the needs of those who have undergone a termination. But individual ministers can always seek to devise a form of prayer that meets the specific needs of a family.

Multiple birth and bereavement

The difficulties of infant bereavement are exacerbated when the mother has two (or more) babies and one (or more) dies. The feelings described above still apply, but there is the added complication of knowing that one (or more) baby is still alive. It is a time of both celebration and mourning. Again, the insensitive "well, you've still got one baby" doesn't ease the sense of loss and grief. It is a mistake to think that quadruplets can become triplets, or triplets become twins, or twins become a single child. But one has to recognize the death of the child (or children) and not act and speak as though they were still alive or, conversely, that they had never lived.

I recall one occasion when baptizing two surviving triplets, inviting the family to pause and remember the triplet who had died, calling her by name. Those present found this very helpful and comforting to know that she had not been forgotten.

As with the birth of a single child, the loss of one or more babies and the survival of others, can bring a real sense of failure. The avoidance of any mention of the dead child(ren) by well-meaning family and friends only adds to this sense of loss and isolation. Often the avoidance of mentioning the deceased child is an attempt not to distress the parent(s) further and because those around don't feel able to deal with grief in such situations.

Our task as helpers is to allow the parent(s) to express their feelings and talk about the child(ren) who have died. Talking about the loss can and does bring a form of comfort at a very distressing and traumatic time. We need to remember that for parents who lose a child while another survives, each birthday is also an anniversary of a death. It can take a long time to adjust to the mixed feelings of both celebration and mourning.

Childhood bereavement

Like infant bereavement, the death of a child (I'm thinking in terms of children from 1 year old to late teens) is a very complex and demanding area. Parents generally expect their children to outlive them and when a child dies, there is not only their grief to minister to, but also the grief of siblings, grandparents, and peers of the deceased.

When ministering to bereaved parents we should always be aware of any siblings there might be and how the death of a brother or sister has affected them. It is all too easy to concentrate on the parents' grief and to ignore the grief of the siblings. This may well be because we are aware of our lack of knowledge as to how to minister to them. Adults are not always the ones to whom young people turn in their grief; they tend to seek out their peers in order to express their emotions.

A 17-year-old boy died suddenly of an

aneurysm one Friday evening. His friends (my son among them) were not able to talk about their grief to the adults around: teachers or parents. It was only on Monday morning on their return to school when they were able to talk to each other, that they began to come to terms with their feelings. To have over a hundred high school students at the funeral service was quite a moving occasion.

The way in which we explain what we believe happens at death will depend to a large extent on the age and understanding of the bereaved child(ren) involved. To a young child it may only be necessary to say that the person who has died is in heaven, while to a teenager, a more adult reasoning can be used. Each will assimilate the information given and what they pick up from their families around them, and from their own idea of what has happened and how best they might understand it.

The watchword in the situations dealt with in this and the previous chapter should always be "sensitivity."

Seven

Today's Funeral

We are faced today with a generation that is, to some extent and generally speaking, ignorant of the Scriptures and, to some degree, of the Church's traditions. In recent years there has been a decline in churchgoing, and the changes in schools' Religious Education syllabuses have only served to increase this fall of Christianity from the social awareness. This, I believe, is due in part to the increasing multicultural nature of society and also in part to the increase in secularism. There is a tendency among some people to see secularism as the only viable alternative to those sections of organized religions that appear to hold an extremist point of view. Such a view seems to create, within those concerned, a need to discover or create their own understanding of spirituality. This does not mean that there has been a decline in spirituality, but rather that there has been a rise in implicit spirituality, what I referred to in the introduction as "folk religion."

We can see this implicit spirituality displayed in the reaction of people to some of the disasters that have shaken our world in recent decades, such as the events of September 11, 2001, or the many tragic accidents and murders that have occurred in recent years. We are also faced with increasing numbers of young people being killed in action in Afghanistan and other arenas of war.

Community grief may be thought to be a modern phenomenon but there have been public outpourings of grief right down through the ages, from the great public sorrow at the death of a monarch to the grief at the death of national figures like Sir Winston Churchill or after the assassination of President J. F. Kennedy. The advancement of radio and television reporting has been instrumental in making us more aware of national and international tragedies. This has heightened our sense of community grieving and highlighted the need for some avenue through which to express both corporate and personal grief. The poet John Donne portrayed a sense of interrelatedness that can lead to a sense of community grief when he wrote:

> No man is an island, entire of itself;
> every man is a piece of the continent, a part of the main;
> . . . any man's death diminishes me because
> I am involved in mankind. *(Meditation XVII)*

For many people, the placing of flowers, candles, and other memorabilia at the site of road accidents or other such places associated with the deceased, provides an avenue for the expression of a personal sense of bereavement. In the past, just the odd bunch of flowers by the roadside might have marked a spot where a fatal accident had occurred. Today such roadside tributes have grown both in popularity and size, until they almost become shrines. Many of the people involved in these very public tributes may have difficulty expressing the "theology" of their actions, but they are, nevertheless, spiritual acts; albeit implicitly so. They are, I believe, reaching out for something indefinable and something, which to them, is unknown yet is very spiritual.

The place of a sudden death can be the place at which the family and friends of the deceased feel most connected to them. People with little or no "organized" religion may be more comfortable with these more secular places of remembrance, than they would be with a conventional cemetery or memorial garden. This is particularly true of our younger generation. Although many of these roadside shrines are created by "non-religious" people, they are nevertheless created as a spiritual act and are, to those concerned, spiritual places. Their creation produces differing feelings in the public at large. Some see them for what they are, expressions of grief, while others see them as offensive eyesores. It is often uncomfortable when private grief is brought into the public domain.

Roadsides are not the only places where memorials are created. Sometimes the deceased's bedroom, or workshop, or garden shed is kept exactly as it was before their death. Their clothes still hang in the wardrobe, their favorite book, or toy, or possession remains where it has always been. It is almost as if it's waiting for their physical return. These places give the appearance of being a shrine to the departed but they do provide a point of contact, as it were, for one or more family members.

For the more computer literate the creation of a memorial page on a social-networking site such as *Twitter, Facebook,* or *YouTube* is a popular way of remembering. In other cases it is just the simple placing of a few flowers beside a photograph of the deceased on an anniversary.

All these are valid spiritual acts of memorial. Having said that, we also have to be careful that the creation of memorials does not become just a way of refusing to accept the death of a loved one. This needs sensitive handling and might best be done by a qualified grief counselor, rather than the funeral minister.

There is also, it seems to me, a part of the social consciousness that has the need to identify with major disasters. The village of what is now Royal Wooton Bassett appears to exemplify this. What started there spontaneously, with just a few people standing in respect as repatriated bodies were driven through the village, grew into hundreds of people lining the street. Flags were lowered in respect; the church bell tolled and flowers were strewn on the hearses. The repatriation corteges no longer travel through Wooton Bassett and a permanent memorial site has now been erected along the new route. This may well serve the same purpose but will have lost the informal spontaneity and poignancy that was peculiar to Wooton Bassett.

Often the individuals taking part in these and other public expressions of community grief, do not know the deceased or any of their family, but want to say that they feel for the loss of others. It may be that, in the case of repatriated service personnel, they wish to identify with the sacrifice made by these, mainly young, people. Those participating in this way may not always be able to express their reasons as being spiritual but, nevertheless, they are.

This need to express community grief becomes individualized and often manifests itself to funeral ministers in requests to personalize the actual funeral service. The increasing use of secular music and verse reflects something of the implicit spirituality of bereaved families. Popular songs with lines like, "You are the wind beneath my wings," can give the sense of an ever-present and uplifting God as well as implying that the deceased continues as the support of the bereaved. The poem, "Do not stand at my grave and weep" contains some very strong imagery about the eternal quality of life after death. Canon Henry Scott-Holland's poem which begins with the words *Death is nothing at all, I have only slipped away into the next room . . .* is another favorite, although to say that "death is nothing at all" does not always sit easily with the bereaved. There is often some questionable theology in these verses which could be explored with the bereaved. I have found it invaluable to prepare my own anthology of verses (included at the end of this book), which often help the bereaved to make an informed choice of words to be used. Christian ministers who feel unable to individualize the funeral in this way often find themselves being passed over in favor of secular funeral ministers, thus missing an opportunity to offer a specifically Christian ministry.

Some of this secular music and verse can be interpreted as having vague Christian undertones and can serve to represent the "theology" of the mourners. The bereaved do not always have a worked-out theology or spirituality, but prefer to pick and choose from a very wide variety of Christian, quasi-Christian, and non-Christian traditions and ideas. Canon Dr. Geoffrey Walker describes this as people buying into belief without belonging.[1] This "buying-in" may include a very simplistic understanding of the Christian doctrine of death and resurrection, seeing the deceased as being "with God" in a very vague way, or living on in the life of our children and other such indeterminate thinking.

When the funeral service is held at a crematorium, there is not too much of a problem with this implicit spirituality (except in the conscience of the officiating minister), but when the funeral service is to be held in church, there are spiritual and theological considerations.

---

1. Referred to in *Dying and Grieving,* Alan Billings, SPCK 2002.

Eight
Today's Response

As we have seen, there are rites of passage and ceremonies, in most cultures, attendant upon death. A funeral is a form of ritual farewell; marking the end of a stage in life for both the bereaved and the deceased and it can also mark an important point in the social consciousness of a community, or indeed of a nation. When such tragedies strike a community, the provision of some form of service to mark the event would be beneficial to so many people, especially those on the fringes of the Church. It would help to give them a Christian focus for their implicit spirituality.

For many Anglican funeral ministers the only options that they feel they can offer for the funeral service are those contained within the authorized worship of the Anglican Church. If the service is to be held in church then this is absolutely right, but, sadly, in some cases this means only the Book of Common Prayer. Funeral services held in church can easily give the impression of paternalism by the Church (or minister): this is something that we do for them, rather than being a shared experience.

When the bereaved family is consulted about the form of the service then they too have some input and become participants in the liturgy of the funeral. It may be something as simple as one of the family members reading a lesson or some piece of poetry, or sharing in the eulogy or the singing of the hymns. Just as the Eucharist is an act of worship that the congregation do together, so the funeral service is an act of farewell and commendation conducted by the funeral minister but effected by the whole congregation.

We need to remain flexible within the confines of authorized forms of worship and Common Worship services do provide for a great deal of flexibility. Perhaps we, as funeral ministers, need to be a little bolder and interpret the rubrics a little more freely.

The trend in society is to turn to professional counselors for help with understanding grief and bereavement, as modern trends and thoughts in society do not prepare people to face death. There is nothing in secular thought which helps to understand what is happening spiritually and people so often fall back on half-remembered hymns and vague quasi-religious ideas. In doing this, they are trying to "keep the door of faith ajar" (*Dying and Grieving*, Alan Billings, SPCK 2002). This is an obvious example of implicit "folk religion" and we need to be aware of this and to be prepared to work this into a Christian-based framework.

Conscience, for some ministers, requires them to question this implicit spirituality and to "protect" the Church from these and other so-called erroneous understandings of death and bereavement. One cannot help but ask whether God actually needs to be protected by us. Are we not really protecting a form of ritual, which is purely the invention of liturgists? When the door of faith is kept ajar like this, it gives the Church the opportunity to introduce specifically Christian spirituality into what are in effect "fringe funerals." As funeral ministers we need to interpret these "searchings for meanings" and try to relate them to Christian practice and belief. Rather like the early Christian missionaries adapted pagan practices into what are now Christian customs. If the bereaved are indeed trying to keep that door of faith ajar, then we should try to help them to open it a little wider.

Others might argue that to allow such implicit religion into Church services, compromises our spiritual integrity. At this traumatic point in their lives, people so often turn to the Church, expecting compassion and help. If faced with inflexibility and an unwillingness to allow personal expressions of grief, is there any wonder that people seek other, alternative arrangements, which will allow for this personal expression. One can't help but ask the question: "How does this proclaim Christ?"

To bring the Christian dimension back into the

"fringe funeral" requires the ministers to be more thoughtful about what they are offering. Our task is to enable the bereaved to come to some understanding of what has happened and what this means within the Christian context. To do this we have to begin the journey of exploration where they are, which is so often a long way from any orthodox Christian position. This journey of exploration will, for many, take them through previously unvisited areas.

As we meet with the bereaved family and begin to prepare the funeral service, we can get a feeling of where they are on the journey of faith and what their implicit spirituality is. It is our task then to understand that position and to gently steer them toward the Christian understanding of their own implicit spirituality. One of our first tasks will be to help them to acknowledge the reality of death. This is so often denied and wrapped up in such vague phrases as: "He's passed away" or "I've lost my wife." We, as clergy, should not deny the fact of death by the language we use. "Falling asleep" is not the same as dying. Nevertheless, we need to be sensitive to the feelings of the bereaved who may find that words like "death," "died," "dead," or "dying" are rather stark and possibly a bit scary.

Our task is not to bombard them with theology but rather to allow our own theology and Christian spirituality to underpin all that we say and do and to allow their implicit spirituality to find an expression, as together we plan the funeral service. This opportunity allows us to explore, with the bereaved, what they understand by what the Church calls resurrection to eternal life and what so many people can only vaguely speak of as "the next life."

There is no blueprint for a "proper" funeral, as no two funerals are the same: the deceased was, and still is to the bereaved, an individual, and the bereaved have differing perceptions of what has happened to their loved one and what the purpose of the funeral is. As we have already seen, the planning of the service should be a partnership between the bereaved and the minister and will often take more than one brief pre-funeral visit. Some ministers seem to try to cover the whole gamut of bereavement in a few anodyne words that neither give direction for future grief nor comfort for present pain. Paul Sheppy, in his book *In Sure and Certain Hope* (Canterbury Press 2003) reminds us that: "It is the task of the funeral service to map the journey that lies ahead, not to travel it in its entirety."

Many who attend the service will have only this one opportunity to mark the life of the deceased and it is therefore an opportunity for the minister to explain, in simple terms, something of the Christian perspective. For some ministers the one (some say "only") part of the funeral service, which can reflect the life of the deceased, is the address. So often, for the non-churchgoing deceased, this takes the form of a full life history from birth to death, with very little reference to aspects of faith. To try to make this part of the service more relevant it is better to focus more on the quality of the life lived rather than to give a life history which most people attending will know anyway. It is better to give edited highlights and then to relate these highlights to Christian belief.

The bereaved's level of understanding and implicit spirituality is often reflected in their choice of music, verse, and hymns. It can be very helpful for them to have their implicit spirituality earthed in the Christian understanding of death and resurrection. The funeral minister suggesting a hymn that "christianizes" their implicit religion can do this, as can a brief word of introduction to any part of the service that is not specifically Christian. The liturgy, especially that in Common Worship, speaks strongly of hope and this same hope needs to be reflected in the conduct of both the funeral service and the bereavement visiting.

Society (and sometimes local custom) places certain, so-called, requirements on bereaved families: matters such as the wearing of black clothes; the type of service; or the sending of flowers. Funeral ministers (lay or clergy) need to be aware of these social requirements and also be sensitive to the personal expressions of the bereaved. Do they feel that flowers are appropriate or did the deceased want a "celebration of life" rather than a traditional sorrow-filled funeral? Our conversations with the next of kin should not just be to find out the time, place and date of the funeral and which hymns are to be sung. We need to hear and understand where they are on their journey of bereavement, and on their journey of faith, and take our cue from them. The funeral service is an important rite of passage and needs to be conducted in a way that reflects both the life of the deceased and the implicit spirituality of the bereaved, as well as the teachings of the Church.

Paul Sheppy, in the introduction to his book *In Sure and Certain Hope* identifies our purpose at the funeral by saying: "The ministry of the Church at the funeral is . . . to proclaim the story of Christ, setting the deceased's story within it." What better way to show Christ's love to others than to be present to support and uphold those who are experiencing the intense pain of bereavement and to minister the last rite of passage for their loved one in a way which truly reflects who they were (and still are) and gives voice to the truth of the resurrection in Jesus Christ.

Postscript

While writing this book, I had the sad privilege of attending my nephew's funeral ceremonies in Northern Ireland. Richard converted to Roman Catholicism on his marriage to Josie and was only 47 when he died, leaving Josie with their three boys all under 16: Callum, Dylan, and Kieron. The whole occasion was so different from any that I had experienced in my ministry and the religious and cultural differences prompted me to look at what we might learn from another tradition.

Traditionally in Ireland, the funeral takes place on the third day after death. Richard died on Sunday morning and the funeral was held on Tuesday, just 48 hours later. The body is brought home, as far as is practical, on the day of death and kept at home for three days and two nights. This reflects the time between Christ's crucifixion and resurrection. Richard had been brought to the house on Sunday evening. His body was in his study and a small altar, with cross and lighted candles, had been created and holy oils and holy water were laid in readiness. The coffin was open, and family members and friends came to pay their respects. Someone was in the room with him for the whole time between his arrival at the house and being taken out for the service. The idea of an all-night vigil has a dual sense of both keeping watch over the body and of being a time of personal reflection and prayer. This, coupled with a constant stream of family and friends visiting, gives a degree of emotional support for the immediate family. Seeing his body at home seemed a lot more personal than visiting in an impersonal Chapel of Rest, however good the chapel might be.

Richard was sprinkled with holy water and anointed with oil by a deaconess; prayers and a decade of the rosary were said for him. Many of the cards of condolence were then placed with him before the funeral director closed the coffin.

The saying of prayers together seemed to me to be a perfectly natural thing to do before leaving home for the funeral.

Members of Richard's family were asked to carry him on the first stage of the journey to church, which was two and a half miles away. No one was made to feel that they had to perform this sad duty if they felt unable to for emotional reasons or because of physical inability. The cortege left the house with the hearse leading and the coffin being carried behind. The mourners followed on foot as far as the end of the lane and then the coffin was placed in the hearse and the mourners followed in cars. Somehow there was a sense of respect and intimacy about the mourners walking with the bearers that helped to create a fitting atmosphere.

It would not be right for me as an Anglican to comment on the form and content of a Roman Catholic Requiem Mass. I was, however, afforded the opportunity to walk with the priest and lead Richard into church and to say prayers at the graveside. At the close of the Mass, the coffin was sprinkled with holy water and blessed with incense. Water to remind us that in baptism we are made one with Christ and incense to represent the prayers for Richard's soul.

At the grave, both the coffin and the grave were sprinkled and blessed to be a fitting resting place for the departed. After the graveside ceremonies were ended, the immediate family lined up and the mourners filed past and expressed their condolences. Almost all of the mourners in church also came back to the house to continue the wake and to reminisce about Richard and his contribution to their lives.

It would be presumptuous of me to say which of these traditions might be valuable to others. All I can do is offer the experience and leave it to the individual to decide which, if any, part of this might be appropriate for them and for those to whom they are ministering.

The whole mood of the occasion was epitomized in some words that Richard said to his eldest son just a week before his death, "Don't be sad because I died, be happy that I lived."

This postscript is dedicated to Richard Schofield (1964–2011).

Afterword

There are other areas of bereavement that this brief account has not dealt with, but I hope that some insight into the whole area of bereavement care has been given.

Some of what has been said may appear to be unorthodox and some may appear trite or too simplistic, but it is offered from the heart and out of over thirty years of personal experience. The attitude which we, as funeral ministers, present to the bereaved at this most vulnerable and painful time, can and does affect their attitude not only to us and to the Church, but also to God himself. As ambassadors for Christ we have a duty to show his love and compassion to all his children.

> Whatever you did for one of the least of these brothers of mine, you did for me.
> *Matthew 25:40 (NIV)*

Further Reading

Bereavement

C. Murray Parkes, *Bereavement – Studies of Grief in Adult Life*, Penguin 1986

Elisabeth Kübler-Ross, *On Death and Dying*, MacMillan 1970

Michael Jacobs, *Swift to Hear*, SPCK 1985

Elizabeth Collick, *Through Grief*, Darton, Longman & Todd 1986

Personal experience

C. S. Lewis, *A Grief Observed*, Faber & Faber 1961

Liturgy resource

Paul Sheppy, *In Sure and Certain Hope (Prayers and Readings for Funerals and Memorial Services)*, Canterbury Press 2003

Pastoral ministry

Alan Billings, *Dying and Grieving*, SPCK 2002

Theology

Hans Küng, *Eternal Life*, Collins 1984

Words of Comfort and Hope

An Anthology of Verse for the Bereaved

This anthology comes to you with the hope that you may find in it something to comfort and help you in your loss. It is never easy to convey the feelings of the heart in written word. Most of these verses were written out of personal experiences of bereavement and therefore may come close to expressing some of the feelings that you may be experiencing.

My mother's garden
My mother kept a garden,
a garden of the heart,
she planted all the good things
that gave my life its start.

She turned me to the sunshine
and encouraged me to dream;
fostering and nurturing
the seed of self-esteem.

And when the winds and rain came,
she protected me enough,
but not too much, because she knew
I'd need to stand up strong and tough.

Her constant good example
always taught me right from wrong:
markers for my pathway
that will last a lifetime long.

I am my mother's garden;
I am her legacy;
and I hope, today, she feels the love
reflected back from me.

Thank you for being my mum.

Author unknown

You can shed tears that she is gone
or you can smile because she has lived.
You can close your eyes and pray that she'll
come back
or you can open your eyes and see all that
she's left.
Your heart can be empty because you can't see her
or you can be full of the love that you shared.
You can turn your back on tomorrow and
live yesterday
or you can be happy for tomorrow because
of yesterday.
You can remember her, and only that she
has gone
or you can cherish her memory and let it live on.
You can cry and close your mind,
be empty and turn your back
or you can do what she would want;
smile, open your eyes, love, and go on.

David Harkins

You cannot see or touch me,
but I'm standing next to you;
your tears can only hurt me,
your sadness makes me blue.
Be brave and show a smiling face;
let not your grief show through,
I love you from a different place,
yet I'm standing next to you.

Author unknown

A new beginning
And when it is my time to die
rail not at God, nor ask him, Why?
Do not mourn, oh! do not weep
he, safe from harm, my soul will keep.

Sing no sad song, shed no sad tear,
whilst memories live, I'll still be here
within the world whilst in your heart
and of your life I'll stay a part.

Remember me for a little while
and think of me with gentle smile
the things I've done, the things I've said
and if you do, I'll not be dead.

Though my body dies, my soul runs free
'tis journey's end and I will see
through heaven's door, the prize worth winning
no, not the end, but a new beginning.

Patricia Harrison

It's hands that are helpful and ready to bless,
that make all the difference to joy and success.
People need people and friends need friends
and we all need love, for a full life depends
not on vast riches or great acclaim,
not on success or worldly fame,
but just on knowing a true friend's name.

Author unknown

Death is nothing at all,
I have only slipped away into the next room.
I am I and you are you.
Whatever we were to each other, that we are still.
Call me by my old familiar name,
speak to me in the easy way which you
always used.
Put no difference in your tone;
wear no forced air of solemnity or sorrow,
laugh as we always laughed
at the little jokes we enjoyed together.
Let my name be ever the household word
that it always was.
Let it be spoken without effect,
without the trace of a shadow on it.
Life means all that it ever meant,
it is the same as it ever was.
There is unbroken continuity.
Why should I be out of mind, because I am out
of sight?
I am waiting for you, for an interval,

somewhere very near,
just around the corner, all is well.

Henry Scott-Holland

If I should go before the rest of you,
break not a flower nor inscribe a stone;
nor, when I'm gone, speak in a Sunday voice:
be the usual selves that I have known.
Weep if you must,
parting is hell.
But life goes on,
so sing as well!

Joyce Grenfell

Remember
Remember me when I am gone away,
gone far away into the silent land;
when you can no more hold me by the hand,
nor I, half turn to go, yet turning stay.
Remember me when no more, day by day,
you tell me of our future that you planned:
only remember me; you understand
it will be late to counsel then, or pray.
Yet, if you should forget me for a while
and afterwards remember, do not grieve:
for if the darkness and corruption leave
a vestige of the thoughts, that once I had;
better by far that you should forget, and smile;
than that you should remember and be sad.

Christina Rossetti

Song
When I am dead, my dearest,
sing no sad songs for me;
plant thou no roses at my head,
nor shady cypress tree:
be the green grass above me
with showers and dewdrops wet:
and if thou wilt, remember,
and if thou wilt, forget.

I shall not see the shadows,
I shall not feel the rain:
I shall not hear the nightingale
sing on as if in pain:
and dreaming through the twilight
that doth not rise or set,
haply I may remember,
and haply may forget.

    Christina Rossetti

Miss me – but let me go

When I come to the end of the road
and the sun has set for me;
I want no rites in a gloom-filled room.
Why cry for a soul set free?

Miss me a little – but not too long
and not with your head bowed low.
Remember the love that we once shared,
miss me – but let me go.

For this is a journey we all must take
and each must go alone.
It's all a part of the Master's plan,
a step on the road to home.

When you are lonely and sick of heart,
go to the friends we know
and bury your sorrows in doing good works,
miss me – but let me go.

    Robyn Rancman

Perhaps

Perhaps if we could see
the splendour of the land
to which our loved are called from you and me
we'd understand.

Perhaps if we could hear
the welcome they receive
from old familiar voices – oh! so dear,
we would not grieve.

Perhaps if we could know
the reason why they went,

we'd smile – and wipe away the tears that flow,
and wait content.

> *Poem found in the Bible of Jessie Blackwell*

Do not stand at my grave and weep
I am not there. I do not sleep.
I am a thousand winds that blow,
I am the diamond glints on snow.
I am the sunlight on ripened grain,
I am the gentle autumn rain.
When you awaken in the morning's hush,
I am the swift uplifting rush
of quiet birds in circled flight.
I am the soft stars that shine at night.
Do not stand at my grave and cry,
I am not there; I did not die.

This poem is by Mary Elizabeth Frye and was found in an envelope left by a soldier killed by an exploding mine near Londonderry in 1989. It was read aloud by his father on BBC television on Remembrance Sunday, 1995.

The rose beyond the wall

Near a shady wall a rose once grew,
budded and blossomed in God's free light,
watered and fed by morning dew,
shedding its sweetness, day and night.

As it grew and blossomed, fair and tall,
slowly rising to loftier height,
it came to a crevice in the wall
through which there shone a beam of light.

Onward it crept, with added strength,
with never a thought of fear, or pride;
it followed the light through the crevice's length,
and unfolded itself, on the other side.

The light, the dew, the broadening view,
were found the same as they were before,
and it lost itself in beauties new,
breathing its fragrance more and more.

Shall claim of death cause us to grieve,
and make our courage faint and fall?

Nay! Let us faith and hope receive –
the rose still grows, beyond the wall.

Scattering fragrance far and wide
just as it did in days of yore;
just as it did on the other side,
just as it will, for evermore.

A. L. Frink

If I should die and leave you here a while,
be not like others sore,
who keep long vigil by the silent dust, and weep.
For my sake turn again to life and smile,
nerving thy heart and trembling hand
to do something to comfort other hearts
than thine.
Complete these dear unfinished tasks of mine,
and I, perchance may therein comfort you.

Mary Lee Hall

The gift of a child
I'll lend you, for a little time, a child of mine,
he said.
For you to love the while he lives
and mourn for when he's dead.
It may be six or seven years, or twenty-two
or three,
but will you, till I call him back, take care of him
for me?
He'll bring his charm to gladden you,
and should his stay be brief,
you'll have his lovely memories as solace for
your grief.
I cannot promise he will stay, since all from
earth return,
but there are lessons taught down there I want
this child to learn.
I've looked this wide world over in search of
teachers true,
and from the throngs that crowd life's lanes,

I have selected you.
Now, will you give him all your love nor think
the labor vain,
nor hate me when I come to call to take him
back again?
I fancy that I heard them say, 'Dear Lord, thy will
be done,
for all the joy this child will bring, the risk of grief
we'll run.
We'll shelter him with tenderness,
we'll love him while we may,
and for the happiness we've known, forever
grateful stay.
And should the angels call for him
much sooner than we planned
we'll brave the bitter grief that comes, and try to
understand.'

Edgar A. Guest

Extract from "Growing old"
The inward man, the scriptures say,
is growing stronger every day.
Then how can I be growing old
when safe within my Savior's fold?
Ere long my soul shall fly away,
and leave this tenement of clay.
This robe of flesh I'll drop, and rise
to seize the Everlasting Prize.
I'll meet you on the streets of gold,
and prove that I'm not growing old.

Author unknown

When I'm confused, Lord,
show me the way:
baffled and bruised, Lord,
show me the way.

Still my heart and clear my mind,
prepare my soul to hear your still, small voice,
your word of truth.

Peace, be still, your Lord is near.

When I'm afraid, Lord,
show me the way:
weak and dismayed, Lord,
show me the way.

Lift my spirit with your love;
bring courage, calm and peace.
You who bore all for my sake,
so I could walk, from fear released,
with you beside me, showing the way.
Show me, show me, the way.
Wendy Craig

I thought I saw your face today,
in the sparkle of the morning sun.
And then I heard the angel say,
"Her work on earth is done."

I thought I heard your voice today,
then laugh your hearty laugh.
And then I heard the angel say,
"There's peace, dear one, at last."

I thought I felt your touch today,
in the breeze that rustled by.
And then I heard the angel say,
"The spirit never dies."

I thought I saw my broken heart,
in the crescent of the moon.
And then I heard the angel say,
"The Lord is coming soon."

I thought that you had left me,
for the stars so far above.
And then I heard the angel say,
"She left you with her love."

I thought that I would miss you so,
and never find my way.
And then I heard the angel say,
"She's with you every day."

The sun, the wind, the moon, the stars
will forever be around,
reminding you of the love you shared,

and the peace you've finally found.
Bobbi Davies

Footprints

One night a man had a dream. He dreamt he was walking along the beach with the Lord. Across the sky flashed scenes from his life. For each scene, he noticed two sets of footprints in the sand; one belonging to him, and the other to the Lord. When the last scene of his life flashed before him, he looked back at the footprints in the sand. He noticed that many times along the path of his life there was only one set of footprints. He also noticed that it happened at the very lowest and saddest times of his life. This really bothered him, and he questioned the Lord about it. "Lord, you said that once I decided to follow you, you'd walk with me all the way. But I have noticed that during the most troublesome times of my life, there is only one set of footprints. I don't understand why, when I needed you the most, you would leave me." The Lord replied, "My precious, precious child, I love you and I would never leave you. During your times of trial and suffering, when you see only one set of footprints, is when I carried you."
Mary Stevenson

Options for Pre-Planning a Funeral

When a death occurs, families are faced with a bewildering array of tasks to be undertaken and choices to be made. Shock and bereavement make it difficult to choose what is best. Please discuss this with your family. By completing these pages, you can help to ease that difficulty. This document has no legal force and is not binding on families but serves to give an indication of your wishes.

Save your nearest and dearest from being rushed into choices they may later regret.

A prayer for help with planning

O loving God, you know that human life is both frail and mortal. Help us to face the anxieties of death with a calm heart and mind, knowing that you care for us at every stage of life and especially when we pass into your eternal presence. This we pray through Jesus Christ our Lord, who died and rose again that we might have eternal life in him. Amen.

NAME: ....

ADDRESS: ....

....

....

PHONE NUMBER: ....

A. PEOPLE

In the event of my death, I should like those closest to me to contact:

The local Minister at .... Church

My chosen Funeral Director ....

....

....

B. BEFORE THE FUNERAL

After the necessary preparation, I prefer that my body should *(delete as necessary)*:

Be "laid out" at my home

Remain at the Funeral Director's Chapel of Rest

Be received into Church on the evening before my funeral service

C. THE FUNERAL SERVICE

I prefer that the funeral should *(delete as necessary)*:

Be held in .... Church

followed by cremation at .... Crematorium

Be held in .... Church

followed by burial at .... Cemetery
(I have/have not reserved a plot)

Be held at .... Crematorium

OPTIONS FOR PRE-PLANNING A FUNERAL

D. AFTER CREMATION

I prefer that after cremation, my ashes should be

....

....

....

E. THE SERVICE DETAILS

It would be advisable to talk to your local minister before completing this section, especially if you wish to include ceremonies which are not part of traditional Christian ritual. Please note that the length of the service is time-limited at the Crematorium.

My choice of hymns *(please quote first line of each hymn):*

....

....

....

My choice of music *(please state whether organ or recorded music):*

....

....

....

My choice of readings *(Bible or other):*

....

....

....

THE EVERLASTING ARMS

Tributes

I would prefer that tributes take the form of *(delete as necessary)*:

Flowers

Family Flowers only

Donations to Charity ....
Name of chosen Charity

Thank you for taking time to choose.
Please make sure that your family have seen this document and know where to find it when needed.

Sample funeral visit card
(see page 30)

Jesus said: "I am the resurrection and the life. Those who believe in me, even though they die, will live, and everyone who lives and believes in me will never die."
John 11:25, 26 (NRSV)

Be assured that the prayers of the Church are with you at this difficult time, and that your loved one will be remembered during our Sunday worship, to which you will be very welcome.

At ....

....

....

www.ingramcontent.com/pod-product-compliance
Lightning Source LLC
Chambersburg PA
CBHW051354070526
44584CB00025B/3758